A Crabtree Branches Book

TOP HORSE BREEDS

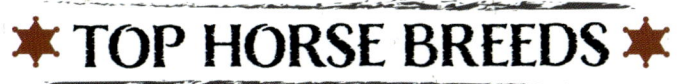

DUTCH WARMBLOOD

Kerri Mazzarella

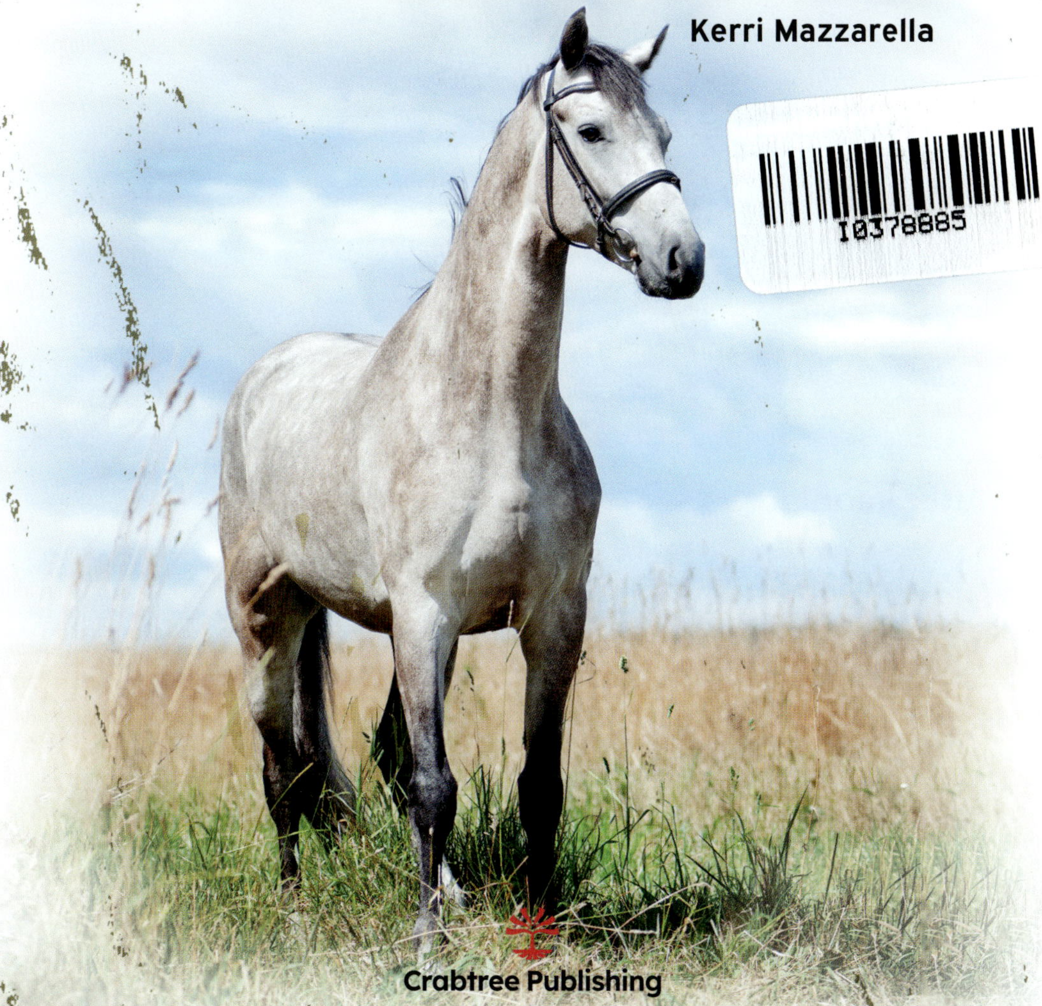

Crabtree Publishing
crabtreebooks.com

School-to-Home Support for Caregivers and Teachers

This high-interest book is designed to motivate striving students with engaging topics while building fluency, vocabulary, and an interest in reading. Here are a few questions and activities to help the reader build upon his or her comprehension skills.

Before Reading:
- What do I think this book is about?
- What do I know about this topic?
- What do I want to learn about this topic?
- Why am I reading this book?

During Reading:
- I wonder why...
- I'm curious to know...
- How is this like something I already know?
- What have I learned so far?

After Reading:
- What was the author trying to teach me?
- What are some details?
- How did the photographs and captions help me understand more?
- Read the book again and look for the vocabulary words.
- What questions do I still have?

Extension Activities:
- What was your favorite part of the book? Write a paragraph on it.
- Draw a picture of your favorite thing you learned from the book.

TABLE OF CONTENTS

History 4

Characteristics 8

Size and Color 12

Care and Feeding 16

Uses, Jobs, and Equipment 20

Cost 24

The G.O.A.T.s 28

Glossary 30

Index 31

Websites to Visit 31

About the Author 32

HISTORY

The Dutch Warmblood horse is known as one of the most successful competition **breeds** in the world. They **originated** in the Netherlands after World War II (1939–1945).

Groningen foal

The **bloodline** of Dutch Warmbloods began with two breeds **native** to the Netherlands, the Groningen and the Gelderlander. These two breeds were used for farm work and pulling carriages.

Gelderlander

After World War II, horses began to be replaced with cars and tractors. People still wanted strong horses to help with some farm work but they also wanted to use them for riding and competitions. In the 1960s, **imported** horse breeds were **crossed** with native Dutch horses to create the Dutch Warmblood.

DID YOU KNOW?

The Royal Warmblood Studbook of the Netherlands is an organization that sets the guidelines for breeding and keeps a record of all the **purebred** Dutch Warmbloods.

Their athletic build makes Dutch Warmbloods excellent competitors in **equestrian** sports.

CHARACTERISTICS

Dutch Warmbloods are tall, with a muscular build. They have powerful **hindquarters** and strong legs.

Their athletic bodies and strong legs make them good at jumping. Dutch Warmbloods are one of the best breeds in show jumping.

DID YOU KNOW? Show jumping is a competitive sport where horses are ridden over a course of fences and other obstacles, often within a time limit.

The Dutch Warmblood has a well-shaped head, strong, arched neck, deep chest, and a high-set tail. It is common to keep the **mane** of the Dutch Warmblood braided during competition.

Dutch Warmbloods are known for their easygoing personality, competitive nature, and intelligence. They are a great horse for any riding level.

DID YOU KNOW?

Dutch Warmbloods are part of the warmblood group of horses. Warmbloods are a group of middleweight horses that are primarily bred for equestrian sports.

SIZE AND COLOR

Dutch Warmbloods are tall and strong. Their height can range from 15 to 17 hands tall.

DID YOU KNOW?

A horse's height is measured in hands. One hand is equal to 4 inches (10.2 cm).

The average weight of a Dutch Warmblood is between 1,200 and 1,500 pounds (544–680 kg). They have a solid build with strong muscles.

Most Dutch Warmbloods are solid colors. The most common colors are bay and chestnut. Other colors include brown, black, and gray.

It is common for Dutch Warmbloods to have white markings on their faces and legs.

CARE AND FEEDING

Caring for any horse is a big commitment. Dutch Warmbloods require daily exercise and care to live a healthy life.

DID YOU KNOW? The average lifespan of a Dutch Warmblood is 20–25 years.

DID YOU KNOW?

Horses often wear horseshoes. A farrier is a person who helps care for a horse's hooves and horseshoes.

Daily **grooming** and yearly veterinary visits are important for the Dutch Warmblood's overall health. Bathing, brushing, and checking hooves on a regular basis will keep the horse clean and prevent any skin infections.

Like all horses, Dutch Warmbloods eat a mix of hay, grass, oats, barley, and other grains. Grazing on grass is also an important part of their diet.

Horses drink a lot of water! It is important to provide them with 10 to 12 gallons (38 to 45 L) of fresh water each day.

USES, JOBS, AND EQUIPMENT

Dutch Warmbloods can be used for different purposes. They are most often used for **dressage** and jumping competitions.

Dutch Warmbloods are gentle and calm, making them great riding horses. They also can be used in therapeutic riding programs.

DID YOU KNOW? Eventing is an Olympic equestrian sport. Competitors take part in a series of contests in dressage, cross-country, and show jumping over the course of three days.

The equipment needed for riding a horse is called horse tack. Having the proper safety equipment and horse tack is important when working with any horse.

helmet

saddle

saddle cloth

stirrups

Horses are powerful animals that can cause serious injury if not handled properly. It is important to always wear a helmet while riding.

COST

The cost of Dutch Warmbloods can vary depending on factors such as age, gender, bloodline, color, and training. They can range from $5,000 to $25,000.

DID YOU KNOW? Stallions (males) typically cost more than mares (females).

Owning a horse can be expensive. There are many things to consider before buying one. The average yearly cost to take care of a horse can range from $4,000 to $10,000.

Housing your horse will be the greatest yearly expense. This can cost up to $6,000 a year. Feeding your horse will cost around $1,000 to $2,000 each year.

Basic veterinary care for your horse can have a yearly cost of $750. Other expenses include grooming products, horse hoof maintenance, and riding equipment.

THE G.O.A.T.s

While there have been many famous Dutch Warmbloods, one of the greatest of all time was Totilas. He broke many world records in dressage and was known to be one of the greatest dressage horses in the world.

Uraeus was another famous Dutch Warmblood. In addition to competing successfully in dressage, he was also known for his role as Brego in *The Lord of the Rings* movie series.

GLOSSARY

bloodline (BLUHD-lahyn): The ancestors of an animal

breeds (BREEDZ): Particular types of animals

cross (KROSS): To mix two breeds of animal together to produce a new breed

dressage (druh-SAZH): A competition in which horses perform special movements based on signals from their riders

equestrian (i-KWES-tree-uhn): Relating to the riding of horses

grooming (GROOM-ing): The practice of brushing and cleaning the coat of a horse, dog, or other animal

hindquarters (HYND-kwawr-terz): The rear part of an animal

imported (IM-pohrt-ed): Something bought and taken into a country from another

mane (MAYN): The long, thick hair on the head and neck of a horse

native (NAY-tiv): An animal or plant that lives or grows naturally in a certain place

originated (or-IH-jin-ayt-ed): Began to exist or appear

purebred (PYOOR-bred): Having parents of the same breed

INDEX

color 14, 15, 24

cost 24, 25, 26, 27

diet 18

dressage 20, 21, 28, 29

exercise 16

health 16, 17

height 12

legs 8, 9, 15

Netherlands 4, 5, 6

tail 10

water 19

weight 13

WEBSITES TO VISIT

https://www.thesprucepets.com/dutch-warmblood-horse-4179058

https://www.petguide.com/breeds/horse/dutch-warmblood-horse/

https://amazinghorsefacts.com/dutch-warmblood/

ABOUT THE AUTHOR

Kerri Mazzarella lives in South Florida with her husband, four children, and two dogs. She loves horses and has always wanted to own one. Her daughter has taken horseback riding lessons for many years. She hopes you enjoy learning about different breeds of horses as much as she does!

Written by: Kerri Mazzarella
Designed by: Kathy Walsh
Series Development: James Earley
Proofreader: Melissa Boyce
Educational Consultant: Marie Lemke M.Ed.

Photographs: Shutterstock Cover & Title pg: otsphoto, benchart; Background and Border: benchart; p 4: @Wiki; p 5: @Wiki; p 6: Pieter Sorber WorldRC: p 8 olgaru79; p 9: genedevine@unsplash; p 10: Laura Fokkema; p 11: sonya etchison; p 12: Zuzule; p 14: Zuzule; p 15: Zuzule; p 16: elisapitkanen@unsplash; p 17: Vasyl Syniuk; p 18: Daniel Doorakkers; p 19: rancho; p 20: @Wiki; p 21: oscarscannell@unsplash; p 22: elisapitkanen@unsplash; p 24: Jaco Wiid; p 25: everydoghasastory; p 26: acceptphoto; p 27: I AM JIFFY; p 28 @Wiki; p 29: Jaco Wild

Crabtree Publishing

crabtreebooks.com   800-387-7650
Copyright © 2024 Crabtree Publishing
All rights reserved. No part of this publication may be reproduced, stored in a retrieval system or be transmitted in any form or by any means, electronic, mechanical, photocopying, recording, or otherwise, without the prior written permission of Crabtree Publishing.

Printed in the U.S.A./072023/CG20230214

Published in Canada
Crabtree Publishing
616 Welland Ave.
St. Catharines, Ontario
L2M 5V6

Published in the United States
Crabtree Publishing
347 Fifth Ave
Suite 1402-145
New York, NY 10016

Library and Archives Canada Cataloguing in Publication
Available at Library and Archives Canada

Library of Congress Cataloging-in-Publication Data
Available at the Library of Congress

Hardcover: 978-1-0398-0943-7
Paperback: 978-1-0398-0996-3
Ebook (pdf): 978-1-0398-1102-7
Epub: 978-1-0398-1049-5